CINDERS

Maria
Sledmere

Cinders

KRUPSKAYA / 2024

But the urn of language is so fragile. It crumbles and immediately you blow the dust of words which are the cinder itself. And if you entrust it to paper, it is all the better to inflame you with, my dear, you will eat yourself up immediately.

—Jacques Derrida

Red Thread

Wind Farm

Cosmic Soup

Oblivion

The only ethical consumer is fire   —Rob Kiely

I adore the word cinder. The instant
dipped red-bitch-gold of the right to die
heard in birdsong, emptying our streets
of petroleum. Bad choruses fill the glittering halls
I have spent my life dusting and polishing
                                   respectable as skin.
                                         Cinders fill
my mouth when I cry, filling the mask
with dry nothings so it billows
many fires started already by words
can't say, my lips are cracked
and scorched meritocracies.
The fire is poor
and funded by life's
particulate matrix.
A melody remaining
that flakes inelegantly
through mottled vowels
and starlings in labour;
motes of them
wild and gorged on eyes.
The person who lit this
initially is gone. All wishes.
We value your opinion.

Cinders

Tossing backwards

my ash balayage, it took five

thousand years for humans

to evolve into prep

at the vanguard of priceless ensemble

bloody glass apples are lit in mourning

so cassideous

I won't text back

I'd rather get a perm

GOOD HAIR DAY

Girlies with veneers in Juicy are letting their masks slip.
    In a few years
Byres Road will be pedestrianised and the rollerblading populace
        gliding
angelically around us will have good hair
and the younger among them will ask
should I get this food my friend has even though I'm not hungry?

Each time I go to the juice shop I feel adventurous remembering
chips and cheese, or
the kissing sessions of my early twenties. It's bad to imagine
        things ending
so we keep posting to ward off oblivion, knowing
the future will see that we had daily life, long filtered

The salt in my food shared oceans with the salt you cried on my
    shoulder.

Podcasters say Love is not a scarce resource. I know happiness is
    coming my way
when I see how beautiful my friends are in selfies,
    their holiday outfits
worn to the hairdressers, supermarket or Botanical Gardens,
    brushing past us

from other lives
to order blue slushies
I love them, they look healthy. I love them so much
sometimes I think, why can't we all find a way to do this.

You only got a bit trimmed off the ends, you tie and untie your
    bike, you take
no time at all to reply, you are restless but full of goodness. You
    rinse in vinegar
        Big salad / Aniseed cola
I taste you. The spokes are broken from absent crashes
to crashes. You are so independent music / I enter
zoom marathons in black and white beside you, myself on mute.

    Later in the glasshouse

        I hush from green of the news refreshing, these flowers
            know nothing
of supply chains and war, they just want sunlight, care and water.
    Many times
I have wept softly in their import humidity
without asking. When I wake from plenty sleep a difference
    inhabits my skin.
You buy me lunch.
My gratitude is a pair of corduroys red and flared.

Now I walk around old neighbourhoods with the warm
        inexplicables
and listen to
Jenny Hval's 'American Coffee' for the eleventh time this week,
                                I went away
                                I went away
into the normal water to not go,
I left my suitcase on a train in this dream
where life was in two caravans
wholesome
and the girl I was also a boy / when stirring noodles in a pan
alone on Friday
these habits aren't mine, I slept facing your face with the silence
of a silent movie inside us, kissing and crying I was so tired
she cut her hair entirely
I saw this film as a child on the telly
in the aching weekend persecution
I was bad as the rain, not listening

    You should eat while it's warm

That girl in the shop was blonde, she was coming off mandy
at one in the morning
to wonder what night is ending in different cities

When you ask me again about food, I'll say yes
you should get it

while you can, hold it warmly through the endless night
as your mother held you
or not as a child, you will bring this
to the person who is waiting for you
in the dream you haven't dreamt yet
glowing potato between perfect teeth
you're up for it, shaking hairpins
        from highlights.

        It's all plotless, but
we ran away from the demand and in doing so
messaging is care. Let me know how you're doing
when you get home
to live with the priceless orchid
saying goodbye saying see you forever.

More tempest than I bring you roses in bed
want more of It, the offspring of a piss artist
soaked in morphine. Because the other life
is pop cultural and fuelled by stars
at the open window rushing us thru
dream security
I saw volcanic heart matters
of other millennia
become dumb astronaut
to ask
why drug users on television keep birds in cages
I know why it rains
I saw the unbridled carcass of a bird once splayed
on my tenement bins
it is not beautiful to say this, but
love I take your hand, baby I take
longer in the morning to remember
who I am
as we are laced with the cumulus infinitive
of skylarks, basically to die a lot
when I am so wet to say it is raining
on Jupiter's baby moon a plug in our ass
electrifies brightly

today

the caged bird says it back to us

More tempest than I bring you roses in bread

as I would fold ardently myself in auroras

and you would eat such thornèd remains

and say as birds are dinosaurs

I love you this big

like garlanded to ask

can I free them from all fossil history

that is bigger than sonnets

pecking at breath crumbs

and the lilac pills that sleep us to rain

inside each other's souls

to permit metaphysical

the kiss in your fawn-heart

is never anaemic

crunching a wild rose

betwixt the moonbread of our dailiness

locked tidally in billions of ice-fire

powering the most active body

in this poem system, drowning

in the lava lakes of your eyes

crying cyclones and the love

that doesn't come down

remains as strangely

ACTING LIKE ARMAGEDDON

rarities of the paradise melody listened in restaurants
with your cellular poised to the oil chord
of many Californias
the angels are not native to the place they are lost
applicants fallen from sky, their halos sung in mezzo-soprano
biology the boom and crash of innocence
is worn bodycon with gold in blowout reality
as you are wearing mad camo to the ball
and sweeping me off my demise, finessed and full-bodied
once upon a highway the Claudia Schiffers of yore
are carried on the Ulysses Butterfly pollinating all money
this season you should wear a bow, we have this wrapped
up in the soaring cost of
living in wildfire classics and the million hearts of the memorial
I touch each one a tiny arcadia in the eyelash of grief's extension
to love subcutaneous mascaras of sadness
only the vocals survive in heaven

I check my email every day like a dutiful daughter.

An inbox is not an oven.

My infelicity is a bad gateau

sulking on the stepmother's polished counter.

It took three nights of poor erotica to finish it, oozing

with chocolate and sloth, luxuria and memories of fornication

in hallways unknown to us, drystone walls coming apart at the

voluptuous, mossy seams. The most infinite animal is the red

sea urchin, mostly because jellyfish are aliens, and the freshwater

rotifers are boring. I bake them into the molten centre

as maraschino cherries of empathy

which comes from living so long in places of low temperature

and extreme pressure. Something holds up the form. It fucks.

The urchin is a swashbuckling vixen

with an avarice for slumber. I too can hibernate

and come back when it seems fine in miniature

to be swallowed by rare cetaceans. At some point

I stopped thrashing at boundaries

and learned to love my landlord's fancy wallpaper

with its arabesques of reverie that other tenants found themselves

lost in, ancient. It was my inspiration for the frosting.

I sent unrequited emails pleading repair, affection.

Someone has to eat this cake.

She said I was a prima donna of the underworld, with my bright red
sighs, not taking my coat off, flipping my hair
in the lusty breeze of hell, bleeding everywhere.

The invoice has arrived, like a rent.

The succulent belch of winter.

I admire your appetite.

Fire is so generous. If we did not have fire, we the warm things
would only be opposite on the scale as all the impossible to say
sorry this is so late & wet. Each lick is so great you know like his-
torical kittens recalling how first they licked a human face and how
it was not like their mother's, but they did it anyway because they
liked the way a person smiled at them was fire and salt. A sun vox.

FORECAST

The sky is socratic so don't ask for that, everyone
always wants a piece of cumulus scripture to take away with them.
Lavish hysteria, peaches.
The human form of falling rain.
                    Taking these futile pictures.
        I write below minus, don't even blame you.

POLITENESS

   This marsh of cypress is solace, is also a street
but for whom? Invertebrates of saltwater, galoshes, thought.
   When I put down the coffee they did not say thank you
my red eyes glow like Ohms.
This is a flashback

to adjacent pantomime, you saying
the latte is too cold, it is never hot enough, I can't
do anything right.

CRYOSPHERE

For icy exception, took Boolean logic to know your arrival
like what is found wetland, formerly, now those portions
of the Earth's surface where water is solid. Hard
yet hardly reliable. Once in moisture flux
and clouded, leftism for everyone
across the globe, don't panic.
Shoals of us made riddles.
On the hard shoulder
of the melting glacier, your pen
dribbles petroleum and wind song, recalls
the black ice which toppled me
once on my bike
in Lavender Town, many ghosts ago.

LIFESTREAM

Tiny units of fire trapped in resin.
This is now possible. You don't know
how long the season will last, or how luminous
to fish for your dinner.

There is a crevasse between the mermaid's formerly
known as legs, it gives a rose.
What does the rose do?
   A rose is opposite to a snowflake
settled on a cube of fire, chartreuse
embarrassment. Both are forms of burning.
The resin inexplicably enduring.
   You are gold in the story
         where nothing is planted.
   Gold is the colour of December
               when light hits the loch at three o'clock.
      This is what happened.
   Which scalar melody had risen in video
the way I feel for you, lonely.
   O bloody Earth
            sirens undergoing such pain
         the destruction of their habitat, I can't say
   this owes to fire, what humans do, their shells
burst at the seams with pearls.
The lifestream
belongs to what murmurs
      a fish does, silt and dresses of merfolk
         strung from inhumanly webbing, purring
            at their cousin crustaceans.
                  Parliament falls.
I like to say it: as if, water

you occur in a game. Parliament falls.
It goes to vote.
You are snow
  tears harvested vulpine
    drift and salt on the road, you are
      minus temperature, imperfect.

ASSEMBLY

We people
a love story, the salmon
have alimony as we take pictures
  of eyelashes stuck to the seawall
    belonging to creatures much bigger.
You are a big creature.
You are guiding us through the end.
  Not in the sense you think, with language
    and grandiose commencement. Dad
  has a hole in his practical trousers, through which
a fish slipped and bit him, now he is gone
    to the beautiful waters
      but I worry because the sea is also on fire
as we do live alone, we the people
have one vote.
  Cleave down the middle our song, popular
but not how you think. A fireball

erupts from our bellies

when you say our name, it's wrong.

In these oil fields

I wear my anaemia like a charm

warning, diminuendo of energy

at the end of which is a bruising gorge,

the colouring of lapis lazuli

how blue always burns

and we are assembled, our hot ashes

trash from mouths. It will start again

but who will go?

FRICTION

This is very shallow. After all

irrelevance, the hot showering

prize of light.

Beautified and stumbling particle physics

falls in your lap.

It is a very great dream when we sit outside tenements

and the boys bring you cups of soup, parcels of loneliness

addressed in their churlish hand

tied with red string.

Lenticular creatures spawn in the pool

massaged by oil

and water, the globules formed

of baby rainbows

we would not dare to eat.

Everyone knows the impermanence of all things

is a reason to love. Save

the NHS. I have a packet

of cinders to share with you the chasm

that I will never be married, yet wear

a golden ring.

You + me come from the sea.

Psychoanalysis grows alongside palm trees

burning on coasts

so you know the metaphor of the iceberg was perfect

but what to do when it melts

and in the dream

only shallow, assessed by air?

POLYESTER

What to wear a dress

made of feathers and roses dipped in gold

is obscenity

for six hundred years

you have studied the relationship between

what gold the blue does water

clarity.

What if recursion were life itself,

overly confident in
hemming you into the story.
We should talk more about love
as like, an engine
following us around and powering
the reason for watering
your dusty throat to make it slip
and tell something.
Ceremony in mary janes.
There should be a sabbatical opportunity
for rediscovering your sexuality.
As for me,
I choose the desert.

TAXONOMY

The Lucifer Hummingbird lives in the desert
but does it sleep
in dry tributaries,
bifurcated and virginal
heard the
white-crowned sparrow does not sleep so much
often staying awake for seven-day migrations
and to think
it occurred to me I have never seen a sleeping bird
except you, little one

in the nested loop of this

typically sultry

moulting

ANGEL TEARS

Falling calcific from iPhone pictures
filling the lacrimal commons of Cloud
and for every icicle damage
of the bronchi flared in your lungs
is also storage

SORROW

Dopamine where art thou!
Medicinal lassitude of passing tempest
        just to sleep
it has been many winters dusting the cornices
    of my heart, inflamed and painful
        to beat, the dust
    coming in plumes of memory
            to start
                    a secret society of particles.
        One day this will be the city and you will be sorry.
    I have considered the pill that makes cats irradiate
        as something to also change me.

One day this will be a city
          circulating
                    the atmospheric trellises of words
                         dying in flammable mouths
                                   before in the air they could cinder

THIS IMAGE

Many senseless borders a mind has crossed
white-hot into the former halo

TOWN HALL

I had to be a lot more sorry
my blood was bright red and tiring
we write letters to people in faraway places
a woman washes obnoxious cups up
every Wednesday is an iron deficiency
there are disagreements about embryos
and the price of gas
the cups are stained with centuries of fatigue
I perfected a generalised signature for the group
which I used on letters to unnameable places
and on tax returns, and announcements
my tasks were largely administrative
I had an agenda
the curtains were sewn with claret landscapes
inspired by historically cheerless platitudes
I pick up the telephone even when it is not my turn
flirting with the head of the community association
the hem of my apology dipped in sauce

The LED reindeer in the garden are fallen,
two of them, twins and neighbours
of the imaginary frangipani I harvest
from Marianne's Instagram
pink as my rage of progesterone
it is fruitful to have three Christmases,
one for every household I am permitted to visit
and with bells on my knuckles or nipples
I give what is supposed of me, passing
at the mirror's deliverance
somebody else's Disney princess virginity
easy blusher, red, red ribbon
I have paid so much for my hair
I wish I could save my mother

LEFT MY CORSAGE
IN THE RAIN FOR YOU,
& ALL I GOT WAS
THIS STUPID POEM

I'm not older anymore.
Sometimes I think walking home, I'll be gone
when dreaming the message

unsent. These coordinates
of pub crawl and delivery receipts.
I turn on my data for you, like no one else

suffused in cheap hot language,
cornflower blue indifference
better suited to rain.

These palaces
curl and burn to cinders
all over my dress. You make
me feel like failed gentrification

I cut and paste
a version of you onto my dashboard
collection of platinum fuckboys

high on the unpronounceable enzyme
peeling me from milky fishnets

everything is faster

I'm not older anymore, I feel pasteurised
by ghosts and the silence
of flashing images,
bad magnolia in summer yards
in a bad shade borrowed and sulky

does it matter that you swallowed my last diamanté
in the taxi back
thinking it was a pill and I'm sorry

CINDERELLA'S BIG SCORE

Autumn is walking home from school
like her older brother
nobody takes this city seriously
park lights at dusk give us everything
pumpkins, Fenders
a hypnotist's riff
we share the same bombed out smile
at the other side of the suburbs it's just as expensive
feeling a key change

. . .

Moustachioed and taken for cash
the wild dogs of the neighbourhood
think you are handsome
you are really handsome
arrested for wearing plaid

. . .

O how they are wolves
pretty in tragic colour tone
adopted by the fabulists

Cinderella is a kiss

It is so sinister to exist here and now
I have beaten this love to the wall
unsure of my sister's whereabouts
complicit in time lapse

PLEURAE

If it's raining, you don't want to be alone
like I want to be inside someone else, someone
who is running, in a hurry to be
inside someone else, someone running faster,
inside someone running faster and faster, someone
who is running, if it's raining

The inferno is so demure

you wouldn't even know its coming.

Our holiday is on fire again.

In your juicy physiognomy you complain about children

playing in supermarkets

because you would also like to scream at random

in the bread aisle, your lungs enflamed

with cold calls

redeemed by vouchers

and the vapour rub you apply nightly

so to speak better through sleep, the menthol

release of articulate particles

an ass for asteroid, bee for bestseller, sea for celebrity

imploring cashiers to take you seriously

even as a tomboy

it's a very bad time.

BAD APP

It's possible to argue that life can throw you some loops

I hope you and your new heart are doing well

The nuts and bolts of the waterfall are starting to rust

I have all these thoughts on Aristotle ...

Mankind is having a laugh

I used to live on a dalliance farm

My husband the dustcart really knows how to do it

Up here, the buses are useless

But at least they apologise, unlike the numbers!

Somebody will appear to fix the waterfall, no problem

In that place, the tokens are blue

They are the saddest of all tokens

On the midnight service

Red Thread

All the poems tagged "anthropocene"
  take off your jackets, take a seat.
I want to fill your cups with golden oil
  for all you've done. The universe loves you!
Drink up and we'll dance on the carpet
  laden with passionflowers and exotic lichen.
I want to fill up your skulls with stars
  so the lines pop off in millions.
Poems, brimming with oat milk,
  cornichons, kimchi: we love you!
Think about the deal, germ couture
  and ethical sourcing for minerals.
I notice most of you don't wear leather
  but your skins are kind of tight.
Never mind the gold is sticky, "raw"
  isn't a question here. You'll find the oil
tastes like the pith of the twentieth century.
  You already counted
carats of transformation, solarity;
  made of theory a ruminant twilight.
Notice we stuck the chairs with rhinestones,
  each one holding a tiny poem inside it.
Rest assured we protect your kin.

I want to refract, to lick apart a jewel for you
and you. Sonnets for a life without plastic!
Sestinas for climate! What was the rhymed
progression of your reforestation
   when the golf course slid away
and smudged itself out on limerick?
   You poems clutter yourselves with fields
and hills and trees and stones and diet coke.
   We shared a look at the rook together.
I want you to remember the names
   like fortune cookies. That's essential.
Take a spin in your chair now,
   let me look at you. Yes, that's it.
Now, hm. The way the rainbow
   streaks the side of your lilted face.

I don't wanna go to the ball
of the billionaires, who in the stars
is your father

constantly pregnant with pearls
I'd rather step from the oyster
and give you one

BLONDE CONTAGION

Taking goose bumps at the disco with you
ambassador of untold story, whatever
we have been told is wrong
there is some
mild kissing, but other than that, it's clean.

In the empty streets of Los Angeles
untold quantum eyestrain
seeing holes in the sky
where holes shouldn't be
putting themselves through biological agony
just to open a counselling service, cloud high

In my ballgown, I have these holes
and phobia;
the city submits weed popsicles
as policy. Want you to peel
my silhouette off bus stops, elicit sweetness
from newlyweds.

Whole intestinal dawn
unravels at the public memory
digest of ice
made lesions in my sleepy membrane, embraceable pinks.

I had this amnesia regarding beaches.

Blemish smoke crush
because you are sad
and I am dancing grey myriad around the rain
for being put out, Lycra
as substitute for irises, my gift
can stretch around

CREATURELY DISLIKE

Exegesis of clitoris
I have eaten the midi
siphoned from loneliness

Phoned my bosses
two thousand unrequited longings
literally in the alien event of fruit

Mingled and silvered by seed's
rheumatic mandible
willed mercy from general red

Devotional handicraft
any tingle of underripe diamond
ghosted by collegial spirits

A Feeld theory, pressed into vinyl
deficits of candour, sipped
from your warm, bohemian chops

I know something inside me is slightly broken
don't wanna sit on the chair
don't wanna spin
don't wanna baby
feel bad, everything is like
burnt juice

a juicebox because
orrery
snake oil, tbh
a loop pedal is calling you
frosty logorrhoea
sumptuous production
avril or the word after april
a single turbine
lopped fruit

half of us are artists
you are the silly perfume
heard somewhere
as bats do see the world in sound
or mistaken shadows

mistletoe

meticulous whist

a three-piece sofa arranged for thee

darkling I run air or like

egg creams for sale

& trellis don't tell it in

televisual the velvet

curt swept leaves

more repeat sunsets

"don't buy garlic"

pardon us of oranges

I like tyres

when I can sleep inside them

coming off the wheels at all points in the weaving

the greatest

loss of signal, compressed

dossiers of Shell

I want to work in the bakery

warm brochures of where we are leaving

ululate nightmare

whose loss

flakes from the blink

all soaked

don't wanna go to the Forge

but you're gorgeous
turn left

I miss NY on Zoom
all I know of NY
forget everything

Rosie's story of the lime foam
coming to alcohol life
the greatest
walking towards malls in the dreams of your children
is a police
to hold ice poles
your hand
is malleable, the dogs and horses
of all the melba toast dieticians, they sing
out of correct
auto-erotic clavicles of moonlight sting me
the city is glitter
it is so
just
the city
in paleo range
rows of houses
my little ones, keep warm

I want useless to feel like the old songs
of Ohio, I mean
falling asleep to the bad lark of TikTok
the rustle of sexts
it has
algae-coloured desires and sighing
don't wanna go to the Forge
don't wanna have to eat anymore
you do everything
scrub turmeric from a fingernail moon

I miss being ginger
celeriac valentine
cut from comrade glossolalia
at vomit celsius
in the tavern memoranda
itching for spring
through a straw

Bubble / Goose / Celery / Lamb / Mall

Yelling / Poesy / Lime / Cordial / White Cat

Lichen / Alopecia / Tarot / Asphodel / Rivulet

Aerosol / Grass / Crystal Cluster / Pomegranate

Lace / Willow / Bashful / Wormhole / Poinsette

Fractal / Dreaminess / Coral Glom / Oil / Seal

ACONITE

Self-immolating wolfsbane, subbing
baby a haunt, balsamic poisonous
got my thumb where, amiable, you
have become a mouth & trembling

before the alternative, angel fired
footnote: I will never go to Costco
where dream is packaged alacrity
in melatonin cellophane, I've got

to go hold, put you on, dressing
for the adult consultation. The hot
chocolate froth of simmering pain
is killing me, licit, you slip

what place an avalanche owes us
vertebra, evermore of the wet hour
not getting a call from you, but I
was supposed to wipe the floor

of Ribena and womb blood, scrape
halogen award from my lashes. In
some ways, softly after all such
abundance to snow on my face.

This cavity has something to show
for it, drilling into the porch of
other girlhoods, I'm sleeping
here, singing. I'm reading you

the long and short complacence
late of the order. If we get to late
base as if having landed on the
unformed morning, terra incognita

below turtleneck, don't. I have
these vessels of red, blue, violet
approximate kissed of snowfire
calcified into sheer finish,

grief flung aconite of toxicity
unknown to me. Median plane
repressing. I love, I binge.
It is rare.

PETROLEUM SONG

I want a car so I can cry inside it
this car is beautiful to me and more important
than its diamonds of headlights
the way I pull up at the water's edge
you grow smaller

As I have argued the peregrine wants to be careful
chipper and sleep-deprived
nowadays poetry's antagonist
holding green calcite to my third eye
in lieu of roses
on the Transpennine the children are twins and crying
their tablets out of battery, they want to go
to the new situation
at the shows, adopted by candyfloss
in whose pink webs their best cathexis
gleams with nascent wings
I have lost a lot of weight in the dream
am less like a person, more like a wound

GOLDEN DELICIOUS

I wanted you two times daily
in the lingering ailment not to care about side effect
ultraviolence of ice, misgiving a Cairngorm
   to climb this last, I wanted you
      a long red scarf in me
pale ethanol, does it make us ache
   in the morning you are all kinds of grass
      like optimism, panic and lemon
         is a gift
   the alarm goes off
in the middle of a desert where nobody hears it
to cut our losses, let's not think of the numbers
   for geometry can be in common also
how I rote learned the shape of your body
like kissing in the woodpile of your mind
   doing all winter what nobody told me
      love poem
      stuck to a love poem
the speed of many trains
I wanted you three or four times daily
listening to 'Venus in Fleurs' on Thursday,
Friday, Saturday saved all the goldcrests
   before this frost

epidemic of the more than borrowed

   peeling poem from poem

underneath I saw cloudshine, taking a thyroid dose

   of something like sky from sky

is exercise to lift here slowly the sunless

turning of apples to new sentences

   concluding with months

   after moths, motionless

in maturity lowland and mountain coniferous

mainly to breed arabesques of genuine birdsong

I am enamoured

to fall asleep with this pleated in me

   the tiniest morsel of glow not due

      to incandescence is only your name

        like softcore

      peeling my flesh of feathers

   and how I wanted you two times daily

     is I want a sort of mist between us

      always to taste of first.

GIRLFRIEND CARNIVAL

Thinking about jade vine and the concept of 'breast'
falls heavy
on the garden's embargo, petulant and conscientious
as hygiene.

A triolet of mint petals around the nipples;

Text eviscerates pastel gradient background;

The girlfriend carnival results in apoplectic spousal
    arrangements ...

Monday's delayed bloom
wears rosé, temporal slump
smelt juniper ... as if

Lightly, I have eaten the spider eggs;
candied blemishes don't add calories.

Recitals on sleep. Jade vine.

The girlfriend carnival ornamented with sparkling wine
is open. You are a water-soluble reader

very pleasing to consider
expanding the poem's virus reservoir. Tiny spiders
hatching inside my liver.

Pergola of seedpod logic, carnivorous
outside the lust house

Patience dehisces.

This is to say, the girlfriend is a necklace of jade vine;
her vowels clack emeralds against us.

Beware of hard pruning.

FIRE RELIEF

This trypophobia of forestry is killing me
with caterpillars lining my gums to wear
   furred meridian, turning to bluey when I call you
do care, measuring temperature of
   lagoon organology   start swelling
over the spell cast. Starts to cool
  I want to.
    Stuck logistical as orange
      I want to go far
  lighting behind me the loves, remembering
sick joy,
   tucking you behind the conch shell of tomorrow
I don't want to return, press hash
    at the turnpike   finance
 close into tabloid
  my ribboning heart
    princessed with want   and wait
  is it okay   it hurts   it simmers
  pandemonium where love is from
behind the scenes of the solstice.
  The rat king of my nylons
     as they come out the washing machine
      screaming.

Ache!

A headline the girl done hard.

It has a hole in it.

Nobody told me

you burnt the coin

I had left in the red velvet

very precisely hidden.

Another petrified motherhood

hangs from the clove and cinnamon bundle

of what

would you like

to tell?

The biggest slice.

Molten centre

of total want.

If I had your cake horizontally dormant

thought. Flambé

at the middle of things, equidistant from all

others you could possibly think of

smouldering

pretty english icicle pastries, apotheosis

elegy

metrics.

I had no arson to contend

with then.

My glass genitalia slid in neatly

where the daily approval of you is a sun
                unspoken, a blue one
also hidden. Shined
        by Alice.
                    No more candelabra.
                        A blue one burning.
            Snifters of golden fluid fill automatically
        where I forgot to dust.
    You pay me merely to dream
of our daughter
    impossibly older than the caveat
of whoever I've been.
                    This nautical predilection for coming
            and going
smoke-wise into hagiography, the oldest
of us
    is stroking my long gold hair
into ashes
of literally angels
conflagrations of their average singlets
                    long gold morning

Petrichor is a very arcane flavour
If you take out the bins, everything will be fine
A season in lethal, apoplectic hobby
Tweezing the long fine hairs of my breasts
I took baths in the tweets of enemies

Wind Farm

I WAS POET IN RESIDENCE
AT THE WINDFARM

Have you ever swallowed a tornado? —Kim Hyesoon

collecting my payment

in leotard, hi tardigrade

polish your gaze in-situ

ZEPHYR

DAIRY

NORTHERLY AURA

Script for a neo-progressive glissando, asset-management

Downwind from spooling innocence

do I ballet

MOLLUSC   NOTATION

My baby

goose soul

is lifting its leg

escape, O suede feathers

to shed

an energy has passed between our lungs

doing its makeup

TUNGSTEN   & like,
blunt tragedy, do you produce this response

all the locals did not want
my unsightly poems near their hospital
flogging earth to a nursery
of tiny trees

RECOMPENSE   SIROCCO   I

becoming this milkmaid

a murderous eructation

peach stain

did you get that windfall

I wanted for you a hayseed

sex fissles in the isotope garden

you are using all lambent imaginary

BLOOD DROPS FROM A NU-CLOUD

THEY DO PERSUADE ME

That time is passé
and lost turbine
            humanity a remote love
milksong
                        turning, turning
                        a whir you are
            For I have learned
                in glossy cryo   BIOCONFUSION

            trend-conscious suspense
to ferment in the boss's office on the floor
I am facing the wall

beyond and subsea gush

I must produce this ode

not concerning a physical element

become devoid

best friend

        "my skin is constantly melting off

                so probably not worth it"

but

do you have a porch?

the snow was an uncategorical love

and fell on the blades

no protocol

      I am rolling around the linoleum

             of miscellaneous symbol

     PARLOUR   LOOM

     ANIMAL   DOLL

      capitalist snowflakes

      corporate snowflakes

      collateral snowflakes

      anaclitic snowflakes

compassionate salt lick

the anxious triplets of shitting music

sun's effluvium overlove, meadow

want mud

a lack

in common calamity <——> dark tourism

simmers in Lago

the dear green placenta

CATASTROPHE AT "HOME FARM"

WARM FOR AUTUMN

APPLE HAMARTIA

you have braided me these golden lengths

I am crisp and perceptive

paid by the hour your eyes

plead emoji

IF HELIOSPHERE

SPIRAL BOUND USUL

KINSHIP SHIMMER

THE ART OF BEING GENUINE

SAXIFRAGE ANCILLA

THEN MIMMICK BUNNY

emulsion of being alone, to

reproduce in the woods
of Cupid's bow privilege

my spine arabesques at twilight, kiss meat

DEVOTIONAL HAYLOFT

a frog larynx
in lucid bone anemone, however it feels

HONEYDEW LABOUR

we are laid off zillennial continuum
it is a commerce of breeze grief
you are so hydraulics, no air

collects   yaw mechanism   electronic
and other losses

This poem is substantially parallel
consent to have downtime
such a mean sea level
of portable social

I might just be a crying pair

IN FATAL PROPULSION

DOLPHIN LORE

SKY LANCELET

LEFTIST PIROUETTE EFFIENCY

A BLUES DIETICIAN

these soft, inexplicable cuts
from leaf kelp and to like
blog about it

the water's formal relationship
gum topiary fault

am I in recovery domain

the OG bohemian

community investment
but take it all anyway
enigmatic elliptical depression

vogue apology   w.w.

A LARK MITIGATION

TENUOUS FAUXBRIETY

DATA INSENSATE

SIGNIFICANT WAVE HEIGHT

The output may be allowed to exceed the rate power's pliancy
Lichtenberg figures of stick and poke
scratch genial this skeletal lunacy, a test case
PROCURE ME!
ECHOLOCATE INNOVATION
MOCHA AURORA / / / AFTERCARE
it stirs inside u

CASCADE DANCE!

thanks, I'm okay

no really

the very garbage of your gentle wave

washes my eyelashes

this tendency to oil

clumps cheap as mascara

a solar-powered theme park inside your ego

    all rise spirals

       impiety

my next role as the understudy of dust

so architecture everywhere is coming home

prosody of the ocean's focal poise

some clip

melodic zeal to the lovely form

admirable in your lap

lyric aloe vera

an appetite and a Levonelle

do not pass gold

your lips taste of salt

economics

ineluctable tremble

The unexploded ordnance of all thought
rope, cone, multi-vortex and satellite, waterspout
and wedge

near ruined pavilion
more watery satin than glass panel hemisphere

nicotine, to you
I hyacinth had slandered
wild under veil initiative

a wage appears
touch a loch

STIRRING

MANDALA OF SADNESS

$10 MILLION FUNDS

WINDSWEPT AND INTERESTING

If there is genuine clarity in the bling idea
congregate by asset trance
brightness in birdsleeve, let this die
I luminous vessel
emptied the cornucopia

in fidelity to habit
deluxe in communal boredom
every door
I arrived at surplus
chemist's repose
cooked dinner

INNER VOX

DOG METHODOLOGY

NONSTOP WHEEZING

>

in the olden daze
price of a lymph node
twirl machine

the world
is a hole

and you are the means of change, quaver, we soft episodic
transmit locale
distress error, you whirl

put claw in there
not how it feels?

GOSSAMER OF ASTER

RISK FRACTURE

INTRUSIVE VANISH

NO MORE CASES

from cloudy pavilion

pull a new star

☆

PROFOUND CODA

TRANSACTION

ACCESS SACCHARINE

ÉTOILE OF

DOUBTLESS REPTILES

platinum

bubble tokenology

Ily a gyre girl <3

(

O

altitude panic

loam tutorial

fate nebulae

comely you turn

the principal dancer

lower half of the yes

syllabi espresso

in solar frivolity

abandoned cognitive apparel of

particle musician

piano lite

expensive nights

the unabridged journals of winter 200020

vitamin shyness

infinite erotic messages

ask me anything angels

)

The relative difficulty

I do this alone

Potassium

soda for the masses I play at forte all the time

the sparrows do hate me

from Texas to Stratton

this is no trade-off, no golden eagles were harmed

a percent of life

I am peeling myself off the future

you are leaving the zoo

my siblings are many

we all are whir

new skin

as pissed

beats

let blood

titular

hope this finds us

MULTI-STOREY YEW TREE

IN THE NEWS

DOING THE WORK

A TWIN SYNDROME

THAT YOU CHANGED ITS SEX

MEMBRANE OF DREAMS

WHIRLFRIEND TO WHIRLFRIEND

IT RAINS ALL THE TIME IN YOUR MIND

I bleed & I nuance so long to confess on shrapnel

finance & yarrow & drink rising my sternum a

syncope of super mushroom & hormonal font selection I like

this one in CGI & moments of emotional intensity override

my internet & I enthuse the world and all of us completely

intriguing & abyssal citation I swallow it whole & lateral

flow anhedonia lifestyle policy alignment & none of this

is good enough & tactile loneliness the blistering caption

I pass so much by design not disaster I buy any wound

& new shoes & soft missives so when it gets colder

a cohort development donut & filled with glitter

the isle off sky & gallery more orange warmer

a halo of forestry suffocates glow & kilometre

the town is a size alas & I tongue stamen no meadow

had logo & I suck lung & align tense mud insecurity

rose & nobody I lick plague & bog myrtle calls me

in a lavender praline field I rise & the alien brine & silent

I search & I sing & I sly would lend a thistle to it

so ferried betwixt them environed skylark & ivy

& coy & I fibre verisimilitude & running

the thread & cotton on nostalgias my wish is flesh

when socialism comes in seminar

I diarise mosses Cardowan a thought in us

a long white polyester dress of the blank & I light
mythology's oblong in agar I lie
folded & I proto & satirise clots
to have written the child in my sleep inside me
the cornfields are lain for harvest & I have it again
her innocence is everything missing
& turned & turned & turned & I turned to you
on a bed of white stones & quadbikes & lucky purple
contracted to write atrocious salt flats
& foams I sound & I polymerise
citizen disorientation & these songs
I write to the vortex of a letter & plan
permission for sentiment & dizzy
as Bloomsbury handrail & Emma's brow
tops eclipse what's next for
arduous pastoral & post-capital lassitude
emissions & silver virus & plastic
alacrity & 2010s made bdsm lowkey
are thee who scabbed my time
is love's practicality, coltan

Cosmic Soup

When we go there, we're all alone.
All alone in this crazy magical hole.

—Christiane F.

THE COST OF LIVING
(CRISIS IN SPACE)

something is broken at factory source
   cloud in your radial artery
      disease of the grapevine

gothspeak young stars in stoner memoir
   many cells becoming honeycomb gourmet
      sexual brain lux of Axel

given to destiny gas bills
   buying up pieces of autopoetry
      let's have a dark lunch

NEUROGRAM

lucky girls encounter their own error

all responses are programmed

to handle it

"protect

the computer's integrity

rather than express true pain"

custom fidelity of elm

imaging nerves anywhere in the body

these events do not elicit

the same experience

periphery

glitch

tectonic

emotional autotune

of mental health

awareness moth

in a Plath burlesque

one thing led to another

I am

It is the season for stupid biography
first you are a Martian specialist, then you make bread poorly
then you go to the Anthropocene Christmas Party with stupid
    bells on
and a lateral estuary of worry. It is the season
we live in peat to perform an elder warmth
unknown to us, ultimate
on the archaeological dancefloor
or moss-coloured evanescence of the way you are born.
I am lovingly human but not really.
If they fail to bring me back to the midnight clock of my origins
I might disappear into the ashen shock of the world's beginning
and do this again, and again
until you learn. It will take more than glass slippers
and oulipo to get me high, although I like them kissing my cold
    skin
so much it fits my life to live
with delicious risk of crack, shatter, shard & e.
Today is a soup kitchen and gold is being poured
in abundant quantity, thick soupy gold
that gurgles as it touches your lips. Will you drink it?
Let's be served oestrogen while telling the story of how I arrived.
Thank you, that's good soup. I was born

with the indubitable fact of my solar capacity
putting humanity at risk of extinction. Not all at once.
It is not my fault. I was born as comets are
to fall
in love with what they destroy. That's why we leave a trail.
Arousal manifests as debris for me, beautiful dust and meteors.
I am all in pieces!
After many orbits, I do expire
in the final boiling of my volatile ice
as blood does after the elongated ellipsis of minus temperatures,
menstruation or sex. I can't talk about my childhood
without electrons or ions getting upset, my siblings
with their earthy longing for a stable form.
It is painful to admit subatomic histories
while at dinner with you, sipping plasmolysed cells of peat gin
and hypertonic passions of making enemies, wearing red
for my art. Tell me about your practice. No,
I can't talk about my sexual encounters with stars.

Redhead of questionable authenticity
all my intentions as a pre-Raphaelite sprite are sincere
ready for anything
pretending my tongue is thornèd,
pierced by the greatest misanthrope
I like the colour that nobody else can see
best, softened before Lucifer
in the algorithm
I hate and I love
there has to be more to it, brightnesses
dipping us in laudanum
popular appeal of the muses
your phone is locked
in my hair

MALVERN ROAD

I want to enter attic paradise
of video call and lavender, pouring the olive
oil in your ear. It is a soft, instinctual morning
the cat's disregard
belongs to creased sheets and that pale grey light
of telling our siblings about parks
and how leaves are filling them
as autumn does also
the mulled sensation of messaging poets
to let them know that rats really do
like to be tickled
as science tells us
I want simultaneity
everywhere, all of the time, soft
and regular breath, frost
on the opposite windows
it is smaller than human hearing
your poor sweet cough
the way our friends send photos
of poems in bad resolution
lozenges of sanitised hour
start me crying, red, brown, gold and grey

there is something wrong with me, planetary

and tapered of sleep

I worship Selene

ringing the bell

WOUND WALL

Answer it! His installation
burns the apartment in trappings of light
opera tonguing the hour.
It's impossible.
The application.
A compact: powder, lipstick, no more secrets.
Isabelle Huppert wears a scorched dress but departs from the
taxi perfect.
I wear the invisible chignon
in many restaurants; a necklace of pearls, the double-breasted
freshwater retreat, rooms
of red walls resembling meat. Somebody once sat here, leather-
bound
folding a purse. Sorry,
you must be hungry. The arrangement of pallor
such that we couldn't stay.
If I could eat now
I could bear the mouth moves, for my last meal
with the blood running down a nylon leg, returning to marbled
arousal.
Upside down, tomorrow
is running out the blood of us
and I do not pretend to know the unbearable warm devastation.

Sweet pills. Beauty
pulls the tablecloth, rides through the night.
A breakable crystal. My kingdom! Sleep well.
I have taken a shower a man and woman
and papered the cracks with intangibles.
I will call you, in my ashen yield
style unmatched memory is everything.
If you have loved someone
in the fever, kissing my ear, please
don't leave. Her clavicle is visible.

SEWING INTO MY ARM
ANOTHER POEM WITH
YOUR NAME IN IT

I was a heap of crying materials, the same person
you once loved and fucked into a pile of leaves
our shame released as spores
couldn't hold it together

I will let my cuticles heal.

Pyrrhic rain is the new cancellation.

I paint my nails incalculable sunsets. Eros

lives in nitrocellulose, leaving red streaks

in the righthand margin. We push our belonging

into boxes, we haul upstairs, we fold our bodies

inside more bodies. When I got sick, you kissed each finger

of each of my hands, thinking I was seaweed, until each

grew a ring, a band of solar pulse

the dads called gold.

I would photosynthesise birdcall, whole emporia

of thalassic longevity, jellyfish medusae suspended from plastic
    hooks

and sold as *biologically immortal*. Water

spits its gilt on our frozen lids, melting through cardboard.

There were life stages we missed, others we longed for

in figures of not-being-seen

or delivered at dawn to the rich and famous survivors.

I, slaughterer of dust,

by the stunning rain of nothing

died. Ripe capsules

of dissilient grape remain here, inebriate

molecules of the lovemade, as if

touch was yet possible

polished of glass, blobular and changed

into the sexually immature polyp.

f   o   r

                                        a   g

i   n   g

        ( )

                        b   l   i   t   h   e

                                                            ( )

                        d   o   ll   a r

                                                        l
                                                        i
                                                        g
                                                        h
                                                        t

                                ( )

                        s   a l t

                        o

                            v

                                u

                                    m

( )

t   e

r m   i   n

a l

c

( )

l   i

m a

x

Time bolt
mellifluous hyperticks of
dendrites caught in my oesophagus
blessed irises multiplied on film reel
around the solar point of psychosis
god spot oil on your lovely denim
anarchism of all twilight walks
we are trace shimmer
of human crushing my carbon
hearts put to work in a cop car
flaring with illegal ideas
in bright implacable
cash sisterhood
printed shine at the library
blink comparator
eleven years old and
calling from anywhere
a sort of heirloom gloriole
in moderately eccentric orbit
one hour lost to the icicle turnstile
like being counselled
in the giant identity crisis

SHINE

I could tell you about the many times your voice has walked me
    home, tendering
rainbow candy, how it is now the changing of the season still a
    thing
apparently—just look at the amaryllis family, every yellow
has its changing bloom
and I am just a child:
all discord, no reason
twice the age of when I first assumed I'd be claimed by Martians,
    overnight
in the amenorrhea of my little secret.
Wish I could tell you about
the fairground, blasting the Black Eyed Peas on Glasgow Green
it's changeless, preheating myself to eat some feeling
just at the neon tip of your voice in memory, a sort of floss,
there's no awkwardness
just the gift
walking through pebbledash estates,
lonesome public parks and the truism of the rarity of play,
unsupervised in music and rubber mulch to prevent injury
I swung from the self-same cord of omniscience
to write this devoted to
your poems salvaged from the web archive, still stringy

with cloud

and cancellation.

I know not what pop song still plays in my ears

so gladly, weird to be anything

to search your name

permalinked to a pearl

shelling crass midi xylophone sweating geometry

with my tongue in your neck

to forget

a feeling, no

a picture

taken of the twisters emitting phone charge

and screaming elation

I keep my distance

I can only be cool, and bedsore

and wholly another story

cutting dumb eulogy all the same

I'm known, almost hungry.

Blood flirts youth pale at picnics.

To keep loving is to be in grief,

when I say goodbye in a small way

watering the grief to grow more

and even more beautiful, like girl hair.

The last thing to seem possible:

make a profile shine from irony.

My fuck expires into phone light and slow passing

transinfinite freeway, tell me what it means
to find multiplying in cells the wrong colour
replacing my Hollywood with Notley
the aspect ratio of love's premonition
financial collapse, a platinum skull of New York,
dear green time capsule sweetly releasing.
I saw a tiny mouse opposite Bellgrove
and full moon in Libra the radical hospitality
microneedling its scar reduction
to like take quaaludes at the clootie shrine
because impermanence
leaves me desirous of sleep
the astigmatism diagnosed recently
means I live daily with refractive error,
a frisson of anachronism and low-rise jeans
the reason for two matching bruises on cach of my hips.
Make a wish.
You are happier
but I am sadder, calmer,
more destroyed. Please let me be
not the new sore person
worse than being anyone
unsure of how anybody could touch me
ever again, reaction shot,
writing a letter to how it feels to be seen
was I ever really

I mean, sitting up late for your call
just wanting to stream and stream.
If I had an artist to whom I owe death it's flowers.
Seems stupid. Violet-black
orgulous blooms, lost thong, tumescent poems,
bad magazines bought at the hospital.
My heart slackens at the screen love
nobody sees again: pink breeze, the tulip wood.
Raging collagen.
If I could just swing down this golden chain and unclasp
the locket of your voice—love
—entirely the jelly of new blood inside me
you said you didn't mind
assuming a listening posture to imitate slumber
we still fit together
harnessing cinders
our warmer limbs
cried out the light, the strip fire
puts me to bed
with your voice-acid of vulnerable objects
dissolving my dreams into the largesse
of blue concussion, the calamity of email,
a snowflake made of plexiglass
computerised tomography
this era of institutional polyamory
look after yourself

marking in the Starbucks at the back of my mind

many things got better with words, sultry

and combustible

literacy of how a thing ends

the spore polis of my timeblindness

amorous egress

just give me a truth that might survive

odysseying after blood tests

so Lara to be legal, shrine-like

the sibling rivalry of language

too tired to see the lunar eclipse

on an alkaline diet of watching the outside

drift from witness

I miss you

lucid, cute

what more can I do

never cared for the gravitational
pull of the future
slamming me somehow
into the flowerbed
when all our worries about work
used up the weedkiller and I was quite drunk
in your superarms, all of you
put your energy into remembering
10 billion small bright girls

Oblivion

Almost before it started blue the snow was gone
stunning and crystalline into a post-it written over
your mother's shoulder, I walked across the river
and south to read with you at the bookshop where
a cake was served, cherry-chocolate and we coughed
from the new rain, it coloured our voices in the poems
and watered our throats with diesel and sugar. Having swept
away everything, the snow knew our shame and its melt
revealed holes. As if not to speak of them
we continued to think about Yorkshire, the power gone out
in the hills our train would sluice, as we cut away excess
curlicues from the tomato plant on Montague Street
baroque in how it had almost died from the effort of its own
abundance, a sole fruit left on the vine
where you had sat, swollen with mornings
and the dream of where to go with the feeling of
anything over. As if to speak risqué
for the want of vitamins, the note dissolved also
in the amnesia of waking to know our bodies
are merely warm mammals: one is cadmium,
the other aquamarine as I do not want
to leave the bed's dialectics, wetly encased in cellophane
and held for centuries in the cryosphere of our hardcore

so that if I leave here, twirling the swab around my tonsils
you will remember my ass and the hibiscus
architecture witnesses the missing, in the ossuary of other forms
our amazing exits are open until they are blue in the face
as the trees were nude until somebody painted them, blue
telling the other trees they were sick. I am positive.

When I stopped knowing what touch was
anaphora of loss, stopped whole oceans
of static positions
my fingers grew chromatophores
swollen into a gorgeousness of spent muscle
remembering how much we had come
to useless neural conclusions, violet-
to-vanta black cement
pouring on habitats of enemies

The insane demise of Nasa was so satisfying
drum machines in other galaxies
held on pause
and pleasure hexagon mass affect
in the spinal chord of the cover song
Kennedy Ashlyn and Cash Askew   live forever
impossible to feel this sad again
wasted, you have everything
an almost mathematical sweetness

GALILEO

My own star sailor

carousing light matter

bruised of alveolar and comely

when the algorithm takes me to higher places

        pale everything

        scared of burning

I observe love, I do it quietly

  I don't deserve to be in this world

tranquillised muscular asset class of stars
the culturing of Venus is pressing against me

DON'T FLY WITH ME

Sustainable aviation my astronaut ass!
Sometimes I look myself squarely in the face of no work
the black hole of masculine reason
in the pull of the long deep thinkpiece
shining with insane light, learning to fly
electromagnetic freelance
in dreams of terraformed morning
mushroom grossing apertures
of dim explosion
STOP—
it's so easy
modifying the contents to include
the author's personal experience of illness, starvation,
acne and heartbreak
in any order, seasonal by way of solastalgia
pulling your spandex pants up
as if to protect from the micrometeoroid aspects
of general conversation, this poem occurs cosmic
and is sponsored by Teflon
the world of no end
is ending
soon you will be at the mercy of a broken police
muscle, his vacuum-packed Huels

and other precise articles

mindlessly scrolling my space mutuals

"up for anything" could be said

honestly without gravity

a washed-up actress demanding Prozac

in the middle of this argument

the oysters are overrated

your heart is an artichoke

who came first?

BABY

What is Mars
baby don't hurt me
What is violence
after all lassitude
What is dust ball
don't hurt me
Desuetude
sunset clause
of the saints
don't hurt me
What is forest
baby
baby don't
What is Sooty
Listen
don't hurt me
or
so carefully
baby, what is
mother's
star surgery
what is love
filling with

octopi eggs
on Mars
on what
novelty sheets
are milkslept
baby don't
violet hurt me
baby
your smiley khora
doesn't
mull over
a sweet cool wine
other planets have also
known us as their young
smallness to smallness
sweeping the morning
baby don't
hurt me baby

All the roadside bars of the beds
I won't sleep in, escaping this rash
of the whisper icicle and how it is sleepless
falling into cool millennia's glittering end, dreaming
one victim from shivering legend, how I longed for a beer.
There are three of us, we are a trio, how I desired to drink
at the triumph of envelopes opening onto lubricant traces
a lullaby of hopeless skin
is kitschy, like a *Star Wars* quote delivered out of focus.
We are in limbo once more with feeling, a glam apparition
my lungs are hornets' nests of lost kisses
whose duration stole all my air forever, I love it.
I was very conscious of being the one to say "shall we go
to the bar" "the house seems open" "the way we look
in the mirror is overgrown"
But you were so hot, all of you.
I dream baby planets in my bed are weeping
marvellous amounts of blood or lava—
do they want my breasts? I am a suckling
child of compromise, got the hots
for one-dimensional villains, feasting on bottled water.
I regret not knowing the real Colorado or opening
visual guides to the bushfire crisis, on the internet

it feels good to close windows

with mouthfuls of sensual ash, gleaned from

the triangulation of gasoline things said yesterday,

tomorrow and today, tabular

like you can take them, dissolve in room-temperature fluids

the negative capability of wisdom, like this is the news

nursing the impossible

lovechild of Jupiter and Neptune

with a wild fund

of words

edging you into sleepless heat, promising saucy aporia

any orifice

afraid our return won't come, just scratching

from the sky's red hollows

PRIME NERVES

The colour red turns petrichor after snow
Browsing Amazon for heaters makes me feel warmer
and closer to space itself, that vast
expensive expanse
of rotational motion
I have no intentions
on these tawdry billionaires
driving bad star ships
It's typo, aka Raynaud's season
I perfect nothing

The terminal felicity of mayflies in oilfields
their voices dripping, laconic with fossils

I have seen footage of petroleum jacuzzis
submitted my payslip to the solar computer

Applied for state-funded skincare, which is
to say, acknowledged my complicity

In the porous economy of shadowmancy's
industrial conduct, applied human resources

To sham metaphors. My feverish
stepsister the female form is swimming

Towards closure. A lake of cough syrup
replaces the tourist hotspot. Agony

Lowers us into climax and bruises
flower outwards across our chests

In gentleness, isolation exfoliates
itself from motherhood's blue robe.

POINT NEMO

remote dilating
vigil amnesia
ice strain of cardiac salvage   spilling hydrazine
    lapidary   plait
mysterium   space payload
    undelivered
      limit debris
low gravity   wound shrimp
     made it back safe
   trash corpus   the outer   nebula
    in ultrasound citadel
     currently unavailable love

Hush now, there is nothing
left to recruit of the universe / murmuring
skyward the unidentified flying Objet d'art
ornaments the four-dimensional plane
cindering duplicate perfumes / on the dark web
ideation point of service / selling us art flux
confusing this flesh for dog tongues of the mortally loyal
flourish of silence in the safeguard between our eyes
first-hand / lovemade quantum clovering
blue glare / of wanting too much
now we are related to aliens and fallen
from union our children set their wings
in the livelihood of the tax credit
forgetting your passwords forever / things will get
harder / richer / brighter / stronger
in dreams of humiliating real estate
time will come crying to your ma's
star treatment / you must think she
stitched me / early onset corpseflower
in 24/7 bloom rotation
failsun / earth pill of the president
singing this tale of the comet
come for you, little

burning world

conflict of our limbic / cartoon attempts

at energy price cap / fear of cancer / genetic

inheritance of statistical probabilities

a sun dial hangs over the mull

lulling us into malodorous solitude

and violet nurture

shale gas of shallow language

and nobody is official / demure policy

dox of the century embers

in thrash metal

flurrying into vending materials

choosing the same old tumour

our noise scorched barbarism of leaving

the planet / don't believe

warmth / wrath / war-

torn freezing to death

is never a choice

like sleep has its

beatific cognitive nepotism

holding us in golden valerian

chromosome remix

to employ our pain in / the hoax

capacity of aspirin / light years away

from each other's ghost software of

having been serviced

to embrocate the moons
in silver morphine
making me ill / lullaby
apologia for breathing / dust mite
satellites / the content addiction
of being anyone for any length of
human time / trembling
as scullery maid of the milky wayback
machine doing idle recovery
pronoun effluvia of our past in plural
for "I'm scared" "post comment" say "politics
is dying to meet you" in hell / gulls
will fall out the blackening sky
cop show of loss
apocalypse could still change back
into the babe that dreamt
selling adjunct lecturing to the stars
for wage minerals eating what's left
crying acid houses of loving kindness
to hallucinate the lousy idea
close your eyes into ashes
until it is over, hush now

ASPHODEL MEADOWS

you must be immortal but ordinary
in the fandom of Hades, I am being replicated
with empyreal exhibitionists

the colour of underworld weeds
unseen to any third eye is the visual equivalent of arsenic
and Vicodin, washed of its violet-crimsons

a marginal species of aphid soul
lives in each human tooth, rotten to the Elysian core
with memories of famishing

our earliest infertilities owcd to the polyglot
who set wild seeds in a pale manuscript
assuming their kin would thrive

in the superheat of the desolate feeling
in the download of dead flowers
marcid with sibylline garments, brass and heartache

NO ONE REALLY DREAMS ANY
LONGER OF THE BLUE FLOWER

And now become fact
it grows in your lungs
many kinds of socialism or breakfast
petalled and fractal insubstance
the rarest of all flowers is the blue apology
slipped into the mouth of the red post box slyly
nostalgic for fiction
like I tell you
a dream, and it burns

RIO GRANDE CUTTHROAT

in the desert the first sun is the deepest

sacrosanct and vexed my snazzy carnelian dream

walking the scorpion your nemesis sings

karaoke larks with kohl or Lacoste

I am sand dune and Cassiopeia

the person you serve as receptacle

for more than lumen tears

my red hair dripping into milieu

my venal aloe a sweet bright gel

in the hot pellucid world of criminal innocents

beyond orange a splash

they are also famous in sheer abundance

clocking in, clocking

whatever we did to each other

strung out in fantasy waters

take off your helmet

becoming the official fish of the state

PARLAY

I have no interest
everything in the world is golden and sore
it is a starfish
can't stomach what passes
for kill these days
a tea stain, a trilobite's small fortune

Having worked for you thirty turns
around the globalised aerosol prison of form
endemic to breath itself, say
we are teaching gym as a gimmick
or seething behind glass at the airport

Say our dating record is 180 million hits
which is to say years, the sexts depicting supercontinents
of wet liability
taking flight

It is our right to do so, in the digest
of forest spores, anchovies and Palaeozoic fossils of seminal
    proportion
we are strong, we are lucifugous, we are subject to copyright

As if in sidereal day you are doing well, applauded
by the society for the protection of abdomens
for that last donation, an aureole
plucked from the head of Google,
please recall when I last absorbed the Panthalassa
and made from its depths my oxygen
it was so tender
and searching

Stronger than the Nasa retrospective
you could fit this heart in a star ship
cut the quantum mustard, be very afraid
of the name of the lakes on Mars, super-salty
like god took a hangover and dissolved it
subglacial into nature cure, the northern lowlands.
   Who ever heard of utopia?
The plaque says: dark volcanic rock
   or equivalent lunar maria, Spirit Rover.
Mars is full of sass in its equatorial region
the dark slope streaks of what sent you
   upwards from loneliest feldspar, crying
      tiny particles of no feeling.
This place is gullied by dry ice, lubricated
   by dreams of human exhaling, the dance
      of once-skin, formerly-rock, fka-meteor.
Hydrogen rich so we could make beer all day
like in Australia with liquid solar, but you
can't carbonate with hydrogen you need CO_2
and the double moons of Phobos and Deimos
meaning fear and panic, I'll have the craft ale
of the latter
to arrive with gravitas and a dress

of crystallised lava, its runs and folds
the drapery of my water
or excess ice, which is the blue
less dusty variety.

 If we know Mars
as I do in my heart to have come from it
wrenched alien at birth
in cadmium plasma, I'm sorry to know
you could not be the first one to set
dumb foot in the dust, as climate changes.
Andromeda garnished by rainbow olivine.
 I am always aged fifteen in this line.
I set my alarm for the morning after
the end of all things in a lovelorn song
of melody's permafrost stuck in my throat.
Look at all the spooky, beautiful dust at a distance
the horrible phrase, 'oesophageal rupture'
which has haunted our youth like a plague.
It is too much to fit this all inside you
red-pilled by the dream of a father
who lit his polyvinyl chloride daughter
on fire
but the flames were invisible, and her soul caught blue
with hunger
he was our boss.
More journeying to the northern lowlands

and returning with rarest clays
made of how cold it is
in your bones to believe in thinness, I kiss
the nape of your frozen brow
interplanetary crockery
we make dust together
now that it's winter
we'll sleep in the garden
wild upon aprons of lobate debris.
During the Amazonian Epoch, there are huge error bars
as to what time is, hyperarid
and dormant moon, many aeolian processes
     of the lungs, I want to keep going
   where everyone has been before like toddlers
you are solar flux and stumbling
for the want of milk.
    The crater is the youngest
    loss of them all
  at war with pubescent masculinity
the sun is boring
     holes in red rocks.
Iron, nickel and sulphur. My pica
makes it hard to sleep, eating it
    until I start floating
           but
  I dust you.

My cycles are menstrual or terrestrial
jealous of Jupiter
            yet proud of the spidering frost dynamics
      tattooed
by glacial trauma of ancient dimension
   favourable to all mission
am I yet
            wanderer of the fever world
      bloodsylvan, unprofitable commons
spread on the sunlit lakes below all of this
      watching us strange thru
saddest perspex
   said as dust
if spherical words surround us
the special melancholia of all life here
rising all the time with our hearts within
   clear membranes
      traces what's always been, Mars
      if I sipped the solar ale of you
         not to speak
         not to sing
         keep warm
      this isn't the journey

In a station of the vortex pick me up and hurl me
on the prow of a ship named for a queen.

—Joyelle McSweeney

Afterglow

And you are melting everything about me —Caroline Polachek, "Smoke"

* * * * * * * * * * * * * * * * * * *

What remains in the cigarette's extinguishing? *Cinders* is a perverse reimagining of Jacques Derrida's 1987 book of the same name and Charles Perrault's 1697 rags-to-riches fairy tale, *Cinderella*, set against mythoscapes of deep time, haunted leisure plazas and terraformed Mars. Lyric, with its spatiotemporal collapse into a simultaneous, thickening moment, is an ideal media for the kind of deep time elegia felt in a burning world. *Cinders* performs that smouldering of the named self: stating, repeating, insisting on presence through the 'I'—cindering into distance, there she is. Derrida: '*là,* "there," made a feminine phantom tremble deep within the word, in the smoke, the proper name deep within the common noun. The cinder is not here, but Cinder there is'. The *Cinders* you hold in your hand is a book about daughterhood and how we are hateful, loving, mournful or fallen daughters of the world, caught in ecological arrested development. Flicking ash into the ocean from our surly balcony. A satire about the gender economy of the starry-eyed men who rule the world and occasionally leave it, recreationally. There's a collapse between the intimate, domestic and cosmic. A pornified body made star stuff, oil set alight by alien flame; poetic debutantes running so, so late in the Earth.

* * * * * * * * * * * * * * * * * *

'To listen to the geologists', writes Anne-Lise François, 'the Anthropocene would be humanity's last cigarette, a name for the fast consumption of deep time'. The Anthropocene, a geological epoch defined by humanity's cataclysmic intervention in Earth's systems, is a propositional metanarrative for the godlike agency and mortal demise of 'Man'. It might be, as François claims, 'no more than a name for whatever within capitalist modernity forces the definitive foreclosure of other ways of being'. Staring down the Anthropocene in the coffee rot of my rented tenement, in Glasgow the tinderbox city, I lacked the mortal shibboleth of being human enough to know. I loved impossible ghosts. My stupidity was beautiful! Man, I loved far too much what started wildfires in the heartmind over and over.

I summoned the goddess Caroline, who writes songs in 'lateral spiralling' to the key of desire, that boiling point where love is the total sustenance, totally enough.

Bernadette Mayer first identified the 'ember' in 'remember'.

Movie stars had the privilege of symbolic emissions, cast in the same old apocalypse, lighting up. I was obsessed by this one way a starlet mouths at the camera's eye: *I adore you.*

I put out that thought on my wrist and watched the skin hopelessly sizzle.

CAConrad says 'I love this world, and my anger is on behalf of my love'.

This little halo of burn re(m)(embers).

* * * * * * * * * * * * * * * * *

Cinders is the lavish embodiment of perishing, like Cassandra her cousin on Tumblr. In lieu of posting, she cleans up. Pulse deletes pulse. She considers a career in hysteria. Love's path of smouldering coals, a poetics.

Writing with and towards cinders, I wanted to understand gender's relationship to capitalist time and environmental disaster. There was the force of language conducting ethical opera on the internet. The pornography of icebergs and wildfires. Makeup tutorials perfecting erasure with the zeal of high theory.

* * * * * * * * * * * * * * * *

Our lovely ashes are packed in pills.

Those who take selective serotonin reuptake inhibitors (common antidepressants) tend to sweat more, and struggle with overheating. The SSRI itself is a pharmakon, the poison and cure for hot weather: global warming, climate melancholia, melting soul sweat of the flesh.

Sad girls of all genders getting their glow-up, a sundew rosette of lure and hunger.

> ... 'the body that will catch on fire
> tomorrow is getting ready' (Cixous)
> ....
> ....
> ....

All the better to burn you to sweetness & blush verse.

Restart the pang cycle.

(eclipsing topos)

* * * * * * * * * * * * * * * *

In *Women, Fire, and Dangerous Things* (1990), George Lakoff traces how linguistic relationships circulate fiery links between insanity, affect and physiology. Through metaphor, metonymy and generalisation, '[a]nger is understood as a form of energy', producing out-puts of 'steam, pressure, externally radiating heat' (Lakoff). My cinders are cast into speech: a performance writing which explores the untenable demands of gender, emotional labour and hospital-ity within a carbon-dated everyday—shot through with elemental intensity. I had an aeolian dream depart from me.

* * * * * * * * * * * * * *

Of man's last disobedience . . .

and the fruit of that smoky missive . . .

* * * * * * * * * * * * *

The Cinderella Complex was first coined by Colette Dowling in 1981, to describe the 'unresolved emotional issues' which hold women back from independence, given that many 'are brought up to depend on a man and to feel naked and frightened without one'. Cinders is laced with that melancholy contradiction; she won't let go of her cigarette.

* * * * * * * * * * * *

'Who would still dare run the risk of a poem of the cinder?' writes Derrida, musing at the word whose 'destiny' is 'separated, consumed like a cinder of cinders'. At the heart of the Cinderella fable is a great metamorphosis into fortune. Catch cinders on your tongue and you will refresh yourself with story: could we be otherwise, ever after? Early incarnations of *Cinderella* see matter charged with magic: a Greek courtesan has her shoes stolen by an eagle, dropped in the lap of an Egyptian king who eventually finds and marries her. In the ninth-century Chinese fairy tale *Ye Xian*, our young protagonist is granted a single wish from enchanted fishbones. Where these tales promise love everlasting as a world reward, I found the energy regime of gender to glitch and stall. My Cinders fell apart in the starlight zone of heartache infinity. To run the risk of cindering is to foster proximity to the flammable matrix in whose entropy we might receive each other.

I wanted to go so far into writing as to literally reach outer space.

I was furious.

My cinders were feast for the tardigrades.

* * * * * * * * * * *

In his striking essay, 'The Fire', Robin Blaser writes of how poetry reaches for world:

> It is, I think, the purest storytelling to try to catch that light—and the difficulty of it, the loss of it, is personal. If I see the light, even

fragmentarily, and lose it, that too is subject matter, and leads to a kind of heartless poem, for it is not the elegiac loss which interests me, but the difficulty, the activity, of holding on to it. Burning up myself, I would leave fire behind me.

Trying to catch cinders is to subject yourself to a poetic Olbers' paradox of illumination and obscurity. You're reaching into the bright-dark void. Even if, as Maggie Nelson claims, '[e]mpirically speaking, we are made from star stuff', the world as such is a fragile glimmering. The universe is just too young for light to have found us.

Goosebumps: strange recognition of spacetime. Shyly, I clung to the symbolic resonance of star quality, scaling domestic frictions up to the cosmic. Alchemical language games. I considered the thick contradiction of writing about crisis from relative positions of shelter. Celebrities eat each other. Cinders as such eluded me, but there they were.

Recall the *Susuwatari*: adorable demon haecceities of 'wandering soot' which star in the Studio Ghibli films *My Neighbour Totoro* and *Spirited Away*. They are subtitled variously as 'black soots', 'soot sprites', 'dust bunnies' and 'soot gremlins', and perform as optical illusions, house spirits or coal-carrying labourers. If they trust the people of their house, they will leave it to them.

* * * * * * * * * *

The black of night and soot itself is sparked, lexically, from a prior shining:

> Etymologies of Black:
> from Proto-Germanic *blakkaz ('burned')
> from Proto-Indo-European *bhleg ('to burn, gleam, shine, flash')
> from base *bhel ('to shine'), related to Old Saxon *blak ('ink')
> &
> Distant cognates also carry such flames:
> from Latin *flagrare ('to blaze, glow, burn')
> from Greek *phlegein ('to burn, scorch')

Linguists Robert J. Jeffers and Ilse Lehiste call this historical alteration of reference 'clearly extreme'.

Cosmic lyricism: the desperate need for a real Outside.

* * * * * * * * * *

> Derrida: 'There are cinders only insofar as
> there is the hearth, the fireplace, some fire or
> place. Cinder as the house of being . . .'

A glamorous metamorphosis on reality television, a cruelly mistreated dreamer: Cinders as primordial girlhood fled from its service to the house of *oikos* set on fire. She was the archive fever of forest, desert, scrub and heath. She was the throb of cartographic hotspot. In her name, I found a solvent lyricism whose dissolve was in mad desire the beginning and end of identity. Dipping my poems in the cosmic soup of elemental carnage, who could have an erotic godspoon of what W.S. Graham calls in a letter 'the celestial porridge of the world'? Only Cinders upon cinders, coming of age in the earthly crater of a fallen star. Hormonal chiaroscuro of love/explosion. Pick yourself up, sparkle hard, be again.

* * * * * * * * *

As I wrote, Cinderella's popular tale of virtue-rewarded began cropping up in the context of various ecosystems. On a podcast, the planning director of a development consultancy describes England as 'the Cinderella of the UK nations' when it comes to onshore wind. A participant in a recent study on peatbog restoration in Scotland describes the peatbog as 'a Cinderella habitat': whose unloved nature is a barrier to care and conservation. I became interested in the figure of Cinders, an affectionate shorthand for the fairy tale heroine, conflated with neglected, long-suffering ecosystems now destined for an upswing in fate.

'Dwelling in the dissolve' of boundaries undone, and broken futures, 'can be a form of ethical engagement' which, according to Stacy Alaimo, touches exposure through 'feminist and environmental practices'. What would it mean to save Cinders from her perishing namesake?

Cinders, a small, hot, glowing coal: the remainder of something flammable.

The word 'cinder' comes from the Old English *sinder*, or 'slag': also a British insult for a feminised person who exudes some kind of sexual excess. Slag is the glassy byproduct of smelting ores, distinct in their strange morphology, often mistaken for meteorites.

'This story begins with a winking star'*

Cinders! How could we care for her stories, reclaim her from the paralysing elegia of woundscape? My own name, *maria*, once identified the dark markings upon bright areas of ochre-red on the surface of Mars: thought to be oceans, known now as deserts. I am named after this primordial scorching of habitat in language. In *Wildfire*, Andrea Brady writes with the ashes of historical calamity and hormone: 'As if the planet / were a woman, living, turned against us', with the lashing incrimination of feminine vengeance. The pressure on that word 'living' and its patient absurdity, like the megalith sexts of Jeff Bezos: *I love you alive girl.*

*So commences Sophia Al-Maria's *The Girl Who Fell to Earth*.

* * * * * * * *

Hélène Cixous: 'When you went away, you left me
with nothing but the sun-bleached world. You did
not even leave me a heart to bleed with.'

In her intimate shorthand, Cinders is a living vortex of extinction
softcore: the gyre of narrative reproduction swirling with blood,
poison, crying salt and cream. The 'we' implicit in the Anthropo-
cene disintegrates into varying degrees of harm and exposure.
Cinders may be in the line of fire, or swirling in the privileged real
estate of safety; cinders drift in ruins, leisure plazas and Styrofoam
cathedrals. Cinders must consent to her own disorder. She's got a
fever dream, just like me. And so after fire, to glean from the IPCC's
burning embers diagram a history of fear and mourning, *write.*
Freud understood the tale of the phoenix rising from ashes as an
emblem of phallic rejuvenation following collapse. In lieu of this
climactic narrative of sexual expenditure and surge, I sought cin-
dering in the tender ambience of lyric's 'incinerated envois' (Der-
rida): playing with fire to write you, my pyromaniac love of cita-
tion, paratactic metabolism, space itself set on fire, catching on.
'Desire', according to Luce Irigaray, 'is our internal fire, our inter-
nal sun' whose burning is the fuel of all 'human accomplishment'.

What particulate matters of the dark come after?

* * * * * * *

Roland Barthes:

(Isn't the most sensitive point of this mourning the fact that I must *lose a language*—the amorous language? No more "I love you's.")

* * * * * *

Lucky Girl Syndrome: manifest your destiny through the virtual babes of the dandelion.

I love them

They love me not

I l*ved all of them

In the hype house wishing for love thereafter: servicing likeability, time flame.

Cinder-sheltering in the crematory of the ultimate poem, what the fire shows of it.

vibration

As I write this, men are digging every road up to lay cables of internet alacrity beyond our need. The particulate matters of future typing indicators cinder our dormant tongues.

* * * * *

[crying into her meatloaf]
Justine: It tastes like ashes!

The girl who knows evil in the world doesn't want to eat. She is told to stop dreaming.

Cinders might be the home turned inside out, an exposed nerve domain. 'Of course, the flesh of the body and the flesh of the world are one', writes Catherine Malabou. Red sinews of cilia suck in and exhale dust in the walls. Who lived here? What traumas do the lovely rats carry between rooms? A post-internet Cinderella clicking herself into screentime while the world burns beneath? Who will save her mortal soul? When will she finish her swiping or sweeping? From what bloggy girlhood's bleached-out prom corsage is the universe confessed? 'A cinder may be dead ash, or it may hide a secret ready to burst into flame again' (J. Hillis Miller). She left a red Martian lollipop to melt on the mantelpiece by the mirror with its svelte narcissus. She left you on read for a century.

* * * *

Caroline Polachek declares: 'the sexiest thing ever' is 'being off-line', 'being decidedly unavailable'. She strikes the hauntology chord. In her dream persona Ramona Lisa, Caroline sings of "Arcadia", passing cars and sun ruins: a place that time forgets. There would be a sweet escape:

> When the world is watching
> I'll take the easy way out
> To wait until you signal
> While you burn the place down
> —Ramona Lisa, "Getaway Ride"

Godspeed the patience of light years, yours and mine. Ned Lukacher writes of the intimate ability to feel the heat of another, 'the sending of what burns within a cinder'. This *telekaustos* is what both 'sustains and withholds itself from thought'. Turning upon itself all the better to remain melting. 'The opening of another topology through language', for Lukacher, 'is the work of *telekaustos*, the sending of a cinder signal'. We receive Derrida's 'impossible emission', where 'mourning becomes telepathy'. Lyric apostrophe is to whistle the live action heroine, look at her go, one of many wolves inside you.

Cinders felt the cinder signal of extinction, this was her calling. The house screamed hold fire on another good morning.

* * *

> She had this dream about a song
> She was certain that it was about a burial
> [. . .]
> She was certain the lyrics went about burying someone's ashes
> And then having a cigarette
> —Jenny Hval, "Ashes to Ashes"

Sweet layers sucking a lyric picaresque through the rogue femininity of petroculture, with its labour of made-up gender and rookie neurosis, lovemaking mythologies of Cassiopeia and toxic soap opera. Her daughterly duty to clean up the emotional mess of the present tense. In love's orbital decay, 'one then suffers poetic scorching by debris' (Will Alexander "Apprenticeship"). What lingers but these flickering voice notes from a haunted internet? I felt the poem stub itself out on my flesh; I looked for breath in the heartwild cast to space, trailing my red ribbon through spiral galaxies.

* *

> There is part of me that trembles
> and part of me that reaches for warmth,
> and part of me that breaks open
> —Diane Wakoski, "Smudging"

Beyond the ouroboros or apocalypse discourse, Cinders is the afterglow of squandering miracle. Hers is an aerosol realism: mass-distributed, dissolving everything. A high femme Anthropocene chorus voice, herself oversignified, siren of cosmos: the book as a clinker brick, holding song. To and from that call: *Cinders!*

(will she disintegrate?)

(is she out there?)

(does she remain?)

*

Then, in place of burning all, one begins to love flowers —Derrida

Stacy Alaimo, *Exposed: Environmental Politics and Pleasures in Posthuman Times* (Minneapolis: University of Minnesota Press, 2016).

Will Alexander, *The Stratospheric Canticles* (Berkeley: Pantograph Press, 1995).

Sophia Al-Maria, *The Girl Who Fell to Earth* (New York: Harper Perennial, 2012).

Roland Barthes, *A Lovers' Discourse: Fragments*, trans. by Richard Howard (London: Vintage 1979).

Robin Blaser, "The Fire", *Pacific Nation*, ed. by Robin Blaser, Vol. 1 (1967), pp. 19–30.

Andrea Brady, *Wildfire: A Verse Essay on Obscurity and Illumination* (San Francisco: KRUPSKAYA, 2010).

Anja Byg, Paula Novo and Carol Kyle, "Caring for Cinderella—Perceptions and experiences of Peatland restoration in Scotland", *People Nature*, Vol. 5 (2023), pp. 302–312.

Hélène Cixous, *The Book of Promethea*, trans. by Betsy Wing (Lincoln: University of Nebraska Press, 1991).

CAConrad and Josie Mitchell, "In conversation with CAConrad", *TANK Magazine*, 2019. Available at: tankmagazine.com/tank/2019/talks/caconrad [Accessed 4.6.23].

Jacques Derrida, *Cinders*, trans. by Ned Lukacher (Lincoln: University of Nebraska Press, 1991).

Colette Dowling, "The Cinderella Syndrome", *The New York Times Magazine*, 22nd March 1981, Section 6, p. 47.

Shaad D'Souza, "Caroline Polachek: 'Seeing Fiona Apple and Björk succeed without compromise felt so aspirational'", *The Guardian*, 13th January 2023. Available at: www.theguardian.com/music/2023/jan/13/caroline-polachek-on-pop-privacy-and-imperfection-i-wanted-undeniable-anthemic-diva-moments [Accessed 16.6.23].

Anne-Lise François, "Ungiving Time: Reading Lyric by the Light of the Anthropocene," in *Anthropocene Reading: Literary History in Geologic Times*, ed. Tobias Menely and Jesse Oak Taylor (University Park, PA: Penn State University Press, 2017), pp. 239–258.

Sigmund Freud, "The Acquisition of Fire", *The Standard Edition of the Complete Psychological Works of Sigmund Freud*, trans. and ed. by James Strachey, Anna Freud, Alix Strachey and Alan Tyson, Vol. XXII (London: The Hogarth Press and The Institute of Psycho-Analysis, 1964), pp. 187–193.

W. S. Graham, *The Nightfisherman: Selected Letters of W. S. Graham*, edited by Michael Snow and Margaret Snow (Manchester: Carcanet Press, 1999).

J. Hillis Miller, *Going Postcard: The Letters of Jacques Derrida*, ed. by Vincent W. J. van Gerven Oei (Santa Barbara: punctum books, 2017).

Jenny Hval, *The Practice of Love* (Sacred Bones Records, 2019).

IPCC, *Climate Change 2022: Impacts, Adaptation and Vulnerability*, ed. by Hans-Otto Pörtner et al (Cambridge University Press, Cambridge, 2022).

Luce Irigaray, *Sharing the Fire: Outline of a Dialectics of Sensitivity* (London: Palgrave Macmillan, 2019).

Robert J. Jeffers and Ilse Lehiste, *Principles and Methods for Historical Linguistics* (Cambridge: MIT Press, 1979).

Ramona Lisa, *Arcadia* (Pannonica, 2014).

Catherine Malabou, "Foreword: After the Flesh", trans. by Mark Allan Ohm and Joel Andrepont, *Plastic Bodies: Rebuilding Sensation After Phenomenology*, by Tom Sparrow (London: Open Humanities Press, 2014).

Bernadette Mayer, *Midwinter Day* (New York: New Directions, 1982).

Hayao Miyazaki, *My Neighbour Totoro* (Studio Ghibli, 1988).

——*Spirited Away* (Studio Ghibli, 2001).

Maggie Nelson, *The Argonauts* (Minneapolis: Graywolf Press, 2015).

Caroline Polachek, *Desire, I Want to Turn Into You* (Perpetual Novice, 2023).

Philip Robson et al, "Episode 9: Winds of Change?", *King Chambers Planning Podcast*, 18th May 2020. Available at: www.kingschambers.com/latest-news/kings-chambers-podcast/kings-chambers-planning-podcast-episode-9-winds-of-change [Accessed 23.5.23].

Lars von Trier, *Melancholia* (Zentropa Entertainments et al, 2011).

Diane Wakoski, *Smudging* (Boston: Black Sparrow Press, 1972).

Epigraphs are from Jacques Derrida's *Cinders* (1991), translated by Ned Lukacher, Rob Kiely's *Gelpack Allegory* (2022), Kim Hyesoon's *All the Garbage of the World, Unite!* (2011), trans. by Don Mee Choi (2011), Christiane F.'s *Zoo Station: The Story of Christiane F.*, translated by Christina Cartwright (2013), Joyelle McSweeney's *Toxicon & Arachne* (2020) and Caroline Polachek's *Desire, I Want to Turn into You* (2023).

'Acting Like Armageddon' is named after a lyric from Lana Del Rey's 'White Mustang'. 'Cinderella's Big Score' is named after and borrows a line from a song by Sonic Youth. 'A Violet Yet Flammable World' is named after a song by Au Revoir Simone, performed at the Roadhouse in *Twin Peaks*. 'Good Hair Day' was first published in *Octonaire* zine. 'Golden Delicious' and 'Evangeline' were first published in *Wet Grain* issue #2. 'Left My Corsage in the Rain for You, & All I Got Was This Stupid Poem' was first published in *SPAM zine #7: Prom Date*. The title 'No one really dreams any longer of the Blue Flower' is taken from Walter Benjamin's essay 'Dream Kitsch', and the poem along with 'Prophecy' is published in *Responses to Derek Jarman's Blue (1993)* (Pilot Press, 2022). 'The Way to Keep Going in Arcadia' is for Bernadette Mayer.

Huge thanks to Sophie Collins, Colin Herd and Douglas Pattison for reading earlier drafts, and to Brandon Brown, Jocelyn Saidenberg and Stephanie Young for so generously sending this manuscript into the ether. I would also like to thank Mau Baiocco, Sarah Bernstein, Alexandra Campbell, Fred Carter, Kirsty Dunlop, Nour El-Issa, Nigel Fabb (especially for etymological tip-offs), Jane Goldman, Dom Hale, Katy Lewis Hood, Ian Macartney, Scott Crawford Morrison, Anahid Nersessian, Tommy Pearson, fred spoliar, Santiago Taberna and Samantha Walton.

This one's for the goths.